Poiema

I am His
"Work of Art"

By Judith V. Peart

Poiema Copyright © 2009
Judith V. Peart

All rights reserved. No part of this book may be reproduced in any form, except for the inclusion of brief quotations in a review, without permission in writing from the author or publisher.

ISBN: 978-0-9852481-9-2

Poems by Judith Peart
Cover Design by Donald Peart Jr.
Illustrations by Jeshua Peart

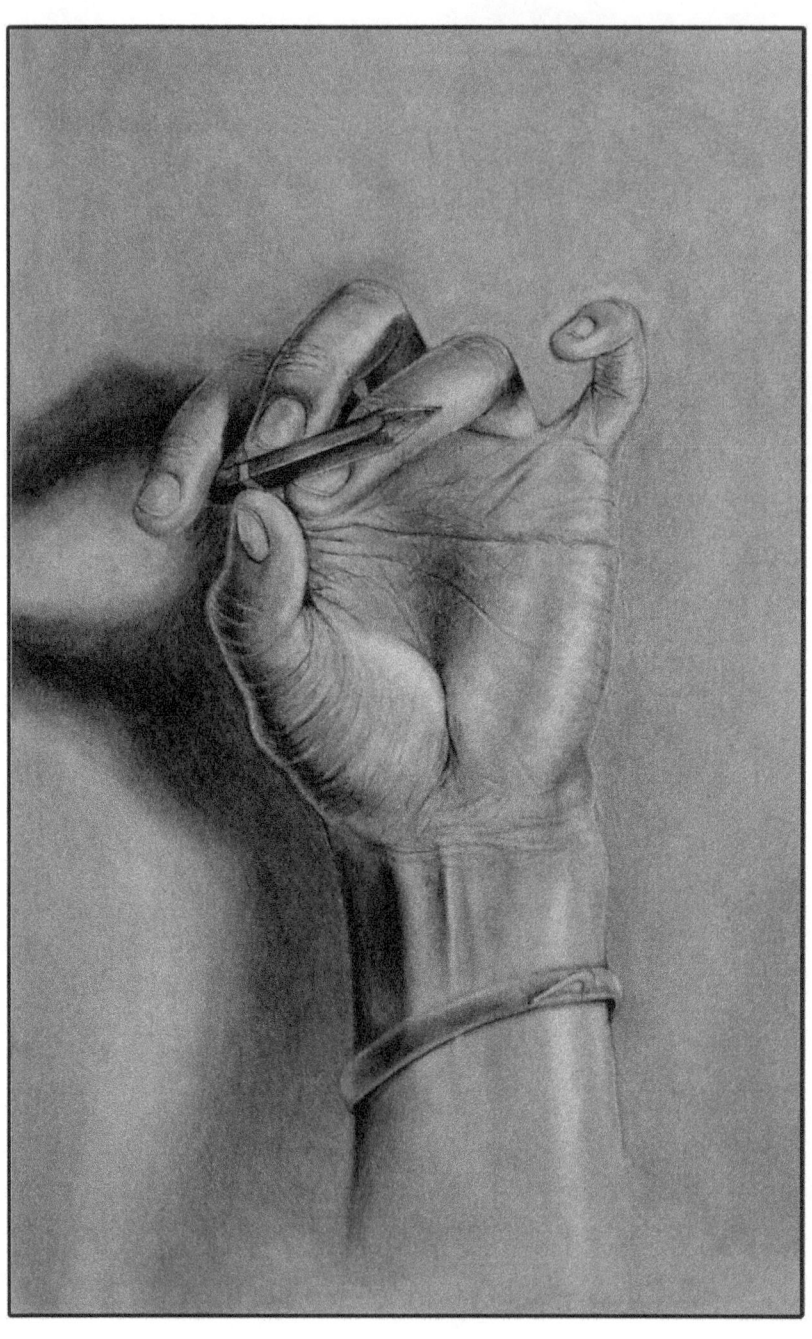

"There is an Artist in every one of us"

Acknowledgements

First of all I would like to thank the Father, Son, and Holy Spirit, for creating me and breathing in me and out of me His Good Works beforehand that I should walk in them (Eph 2:10). I am His creative poetry and I am His work of art. Before I came to know Him, my life had no offshoot for my creativity.

He is my eternal flow, river of life, and prophetic stream. Jesus I will love You, my Heavenly Father, forever. Holy Spirit, You are my comfort, resting place, and eternal strength. Thanks for Your guidance and now is the predestined time for this writing.

Secondly, I would like to thank those who especially first saw in me real creative works of poetry. Thanks Minister Margie Epps, I will forever be grateful for your encouragement to publish my first poem in an anthology.

I especially want to thank my husband Apostle Donald A. Peart who continued to encourage me to publish this collection many years ago. Honey, I finally did it!

I could not have continued to write this collection if it had not been for my church family. *Crown of Glory Ministries* - many of who sat, listened, and were blessed by many of these poems, and heard the sound of the Lord through many of them. Thanks also to Tiffany Kenner for editing this book.

Also, I would like to thank my natural father Harrison M. Tucker who is an educator, avid reader, and a man of great literature, who read in front of and to his children to enhance our exposure to many literary forms. Thanks Dad you made it easy for me to resemble you.

I would like to acknowledge my mother *Frances Gaymon Graham Tucker* for birthing me into a family of art, song, music, dance, design, and many creative art forms. Although she is no longer with us her artistic life as well as that of many of her brothers and sisters had a profound effect on her family, children, and grandchildren, and will for many generations to come.

Finally, I would like to thank my brothers Randy and Jeffrey and my sister Lisa Tucker for helping to support my interests as a youth and teen after the death of our mother. Your example of love, support, strength, and resilience, was reinforced in me and caused me to also realize the fulfillment of many of my own dreams.

Thanks to all my spiritual mothers and mentors, Bishop Sandra Phillips Hayden, My favorite *Aunt* Prophetess Marie Howard, (mom) Millicent J. Peart, Pastor Lula Simon, and Pastor Ola Buie. Through your constant support, correction, unconditional love, and prayers many of these poems were born.

Special Thanks to my sons who are both students at The Art Institute of Washington, Donald Peart Jr.—cover design and Jeshua Peart—Poetic Art Collection.

Dedication

This book is especially dedicated to my mother Frances who was a designer in her own right; my husband and children; Donald Sr., Donald Jr., Jeshua, Charity, Benjamin, and Jesse. To my godly seed, you already know that you are "God's Artistry - His Works of Art" because his creative works have already been demonstrated in and through each one of you.

To my spiritual daughters: Nichole Brown, Sanora Dutton, Trina Dutton, Tiffany Brown, Tracy Dutton, Diane Sumler, Sharone Edelen, and Natalie Keys. And many, many others, "*Daughters know that you are God's work of Art*". "You can do anything you see your Father do" I will always love you all. Without you all I would not have been as creative, because many of you unlocked my heart, my love, my creativity, and a more sure word of prophecy, which was needed for many of these poems. Thanks for your understanding, affection, and continued strength.

Special Dedication:

To my Professors at Coppin State University, especially Dr. Kim, Dr. Jenkins, Dr. Susan Arisman Dean, of the (School of Education) who first heard "The Kings and Queens of Africa", and who inspired the poem "I Hear the Rhythm of Our Children" based on a book selected for the Rosemont / Coppin State Literacy Program, the poem was written for it's closing exercises.

To the African American Community and the students at Coppin State University, I especially dedicate this first poem to you and the second to our children. Know that you are *GOD'S BEAUTIFUL WORK OF ART* and that you were preordained to bring change and the *Creative Arts* to your generation.

Table of Contents

POEMS	PAGE NO.
The Kings and Queens of Africa	1
I Hear the Rhythm of Our Children	5
A Pearl in the Sand	9
The Verdict	11
I Am Not Invisible	13
Exhausted	14
My Friend	17
Tears	18
You Inspire Me	21
Lord You Are	22
Who Can Understand Him	23
A New Day	24
Bestiality the Sensual Man	25
It was a Game	29
Hear the cry of the children Lord	31
Is There Hope	35
Touching You	36
Always Faithful	37
Romance Me	39

The Kings and Queens of Africa

You are mahogany
You are a beautiful work of art
Dark as dark, rich as Africa

Dark as the darkest berry
Dark sweet, sweet dark
as chocolate

Dark as the darkest night
With an array of sunlight

Rich in color
Rich to all colors
For in you precede all colors

Green, blue, purple, red, orange
Yellow, brown, and white

For out of you the nations will rise
Rich are you with the skins of all people
You are African

Darkest of the people
Rich as the richest
Darkest as the bowels of Africa

You are the soil of the land
The land you nurtured in the heat of your spirit
Is the land you were destined to rule

as Adam
As kings and queens from Africa
You will rule the earth.

"You can only create what you see"

I Hear the Rhythm of Our Children

Rosemont Elementary School
Closing Exercises – written by Judith Peart for
Coppin State University - Literacy Program
May 7, 2008

I Hear the Rhythm of Our Children
Paper crackling, pencils scratching, and scissors snapping

I Hear the Rhythm of Our Children
Sitting and listening to their African American Heritage

Reading poems by Langston Hughes saying,
Give me all your dreams you dreamers
Give me your heart melodies
That I may wrap them in a blue cloud cloth
Away from the two rough fingers of the world

Literature chosen to inspire, instruct, and build
A bridge of literacy for the children of the future

I Hear the Rhythm of Our Children
Playing, Laughing, Singing, and Dancing
Looking and Listening
Listening and looking
Our children maybe blank tablets today
Waiting to be written on by the teachers of tomorrow

They will understand what has been misunderstood
Learn what has not been taught
And do what has not been done

I Hear the Rhythm of Our Children
A new generation of leadership who will solve tomorrow problems
Those who will create a whole new world of possibilities
I See the Rhythm of Our Children
As bright as the sun
As creative and colorful as the nations
And as glorious as their horizon

I hear the sound of the patter of their feet
Being enlarged upon the pavement as they walk
Swallowing up the ground as they move forward into their destiny
Walking and Moving
Moving and Walking
Into the knowledge of their heritage
Into their fullest potential
and
Into the power of who they were created to be.

"God has given us His ability to create beauty all around us"

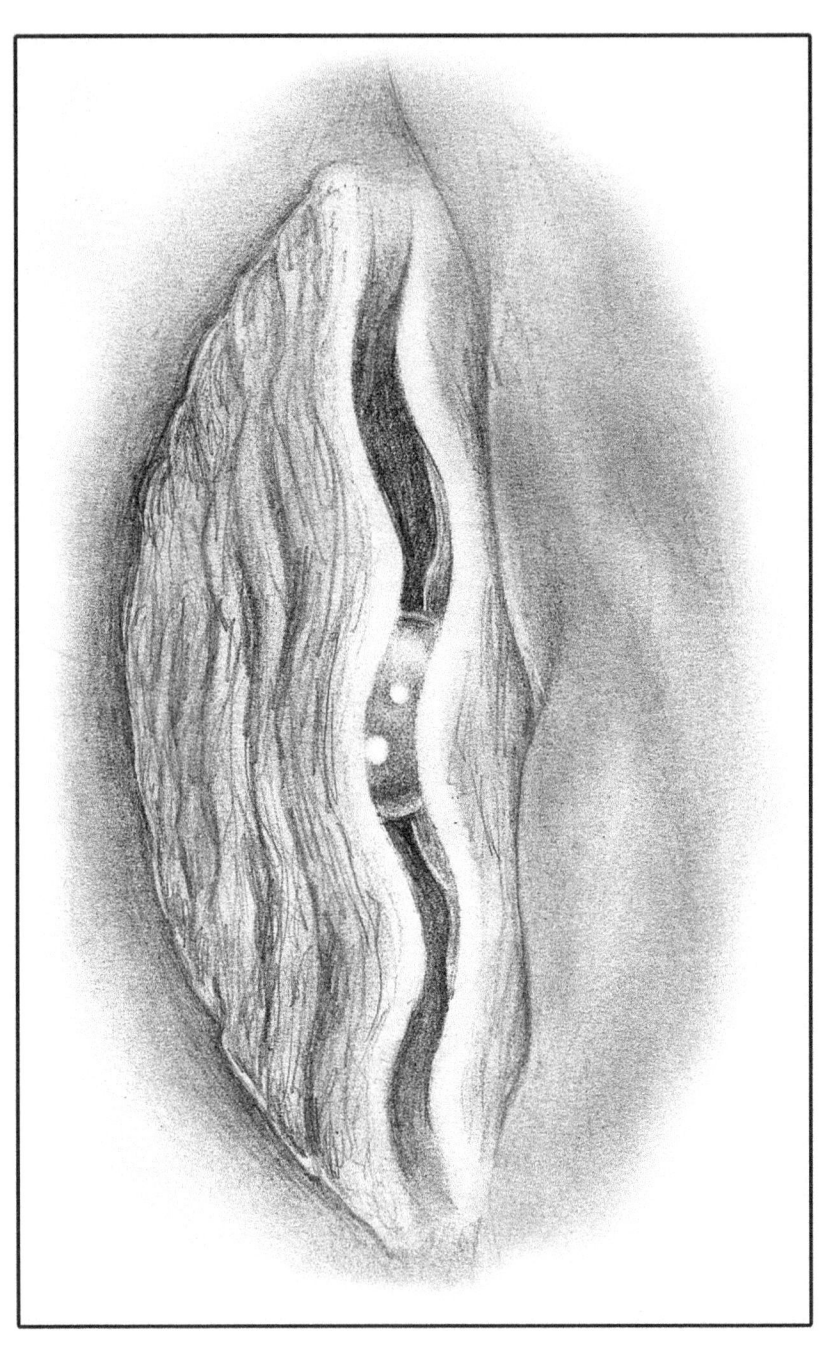

A Pearl in the Sand

As a pearl in the Sand
Hidden deep within
A treasure unheard
A story untold
Like an unearthed nugget of gold
So will you unfold

As a flower buried underneath the ground
The time of spring brings it around
The rain falls upon it
Its beauty is revealed
So the flowers began to peel

Whether hidden or unheard
Unearthed or untold
So will you unfold
As a pearl in the sand

The Verdict

The hammer slams on the judgment table
Every time I fail to decide
Fail to make a choice
Fail to say not my will but thine be done

I hear the slam again
This time it is His blood
Slamming the enemy of my soul

When temptation tries to steal my soul out of the Father's hand
His blood draws the line that iniquity can't cross
The cross of Christ is buried deep in the soul of my heart

Slam, Slam!

The verdict that began at the garden ends at the cross

Lord, I will love you always
Forever eternally
My head is upon your chest Father
I will rest at the end
You are my verdict
You are my eternal decision.

I Am Not Invisible

When I could not hug me, you hugged me
When I could not see me, you saw me
When I could not feel me, you felt me
When I could not hear me, you heard me

Because to you, I am not invisible
From the beginning, you prepared for me a body
Upon the potters wheel
You recreated me
And in you am I significantly made.

Exhausted

Life has many hills and mountains
So remember to breathe
Life has many oceans and streams
So remember to breathe
Life has many hills and valleys
So remember to breathe
Life has many challenges
Although we may grow weary

Always remember
It's not the climb up the mountain,
But what you saw when you reached the top
It's not the struggle that it took to move up stream,
But the beauty of its water falls
It's not the walk through the valley,

But what you may have learned along the way
Although we may tire

In the face of life's challenges
Think about the good out of it all
And always remember to breathe.

"Your world is painted by the pictures revealed in your heart"

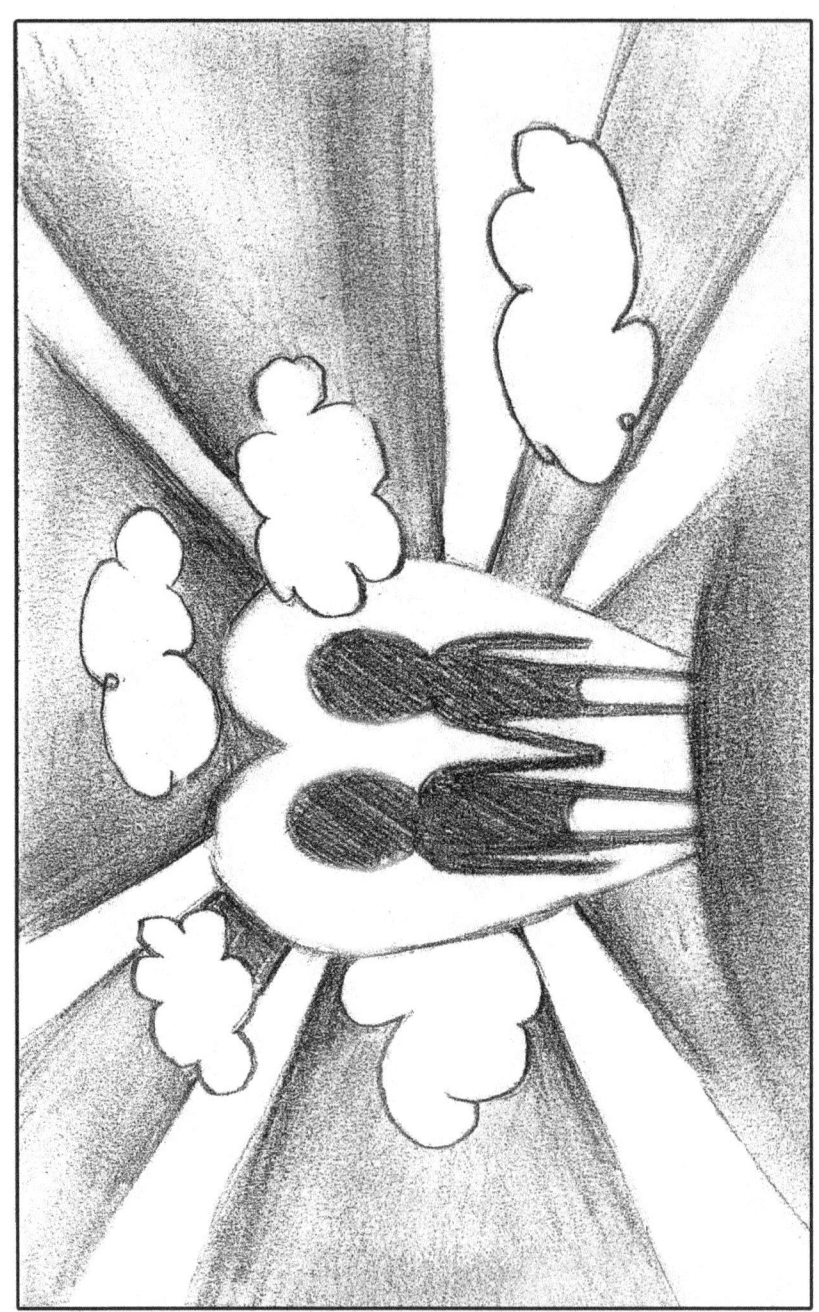

My Friend

Some one to talk to
Someone to understand
my friend

A hand of comfort
A voice that calms an aching heart
Your love can charm
my friend

A heart of compassion
Thoughts of care
Deeds and grace
That's rare
my friend

All along, you've been by my side
Whether in suffering or joy
With you I can't hide
I know deep inside

You will always be my friend

Tears

Tears of joy and tears of pain
Tears of laughter and tears of shame

Crying is what we talk about the least
But what we do the most

Whether they are tears we shed big and bold
Or tears within we choose to hold

Tears remind us that we are not in control
But that life touches and changes those created within it

We learn through our tears that someone above is crying for us
And as long as we live and breathe

We will meet life and the One who created it
And we will cry

"The artist's ability comes from the true Artist above"

You Inspire Me

I've gone many places
I've seen many faces
No matter how many or few
There's none quite like you

I may look over my shoulder
I will peek glance and glare
When I turn completely
I will notice this beautiful stare

The purpose of it all is to indicate
You really care
A care that's so deep
A compassion so moving
A gentleness and love so soothing

A glory so radiant and wonderful to see

He inspired you and you inspired me

Lord You Are

You are the air I breathe
You are the Life I lead
You are the strength I have

You are the one who makes me glad
You are the hope in despair
You are the one who really cares

You are the way I succeed
You are the one who prospers me

You are the song I sing
You are the one who watches me
You are the beauty that I see
You are my eternity

Who Can Understand Him

If you possess the greatest wisdom, understanding, and knowledge
The greatest skill, gift, or expertise

If you possess all the riches, glamour, or glory
or
The importance and recognition we read

To know is to understand
that
He's the one and only seed

In a class all by Himself
In an atmosphere all His own
In a place where He stands alone

No one can understand
So we stand in awe and say

He's the Lord and Master
The creator of the day

A New Day

What awaits me?

Heaven knows

The angels sing stories untold
The destiny of God unfolds

The brightness of His glory awaits me
The light of His glory directs me
The illumination of His glory covers me

I am predestined to see generations foreseen and foretold

The destiny of God unfolds

The light of the nations were revealed
Christ was sent by the Father to heal
And through the power of the cross
The mysteries of God was unsealed

What awaits me?

Heaven knows
The angels sang stories untold
The destiny of God's new day unfolds

Bestiality the Sensual Man

The wisdom of this earth is in the sensual man
Ready to put down others and demand

His jealousy will take advantage of others
Loving himself more than anyone else
He's selfish, arrogant, and aggressive

Twisting all that God says
Reasoning what he does not understand
Refusing God's command

Scorning all he does not like
Speaking against all he does not desire
Destroying all he doesn't love
Setting ablaze his lustful fire

Deception is his way to gain
Destruction is his power

Delusion is his way to sway
As he accolades all that's sour

Defilement is what he does
To spread his filthy pollution
A disease that flows through mankind
A beast full of persecution

There is as Adamic nature
A corrupt man and a beast in all of us
God wants us to love His wisdom
So in Him, we'd place our trust

We must do away with all the lies
And things we'd cover up
And let God and His light manifest all He must

When we allow God to transform our lives
He will annihilate the beast that pants in our heart

God will put to death those mischievous desires
That consumes our inner part.

"You are His creative work; you are the work of the Master's hands"

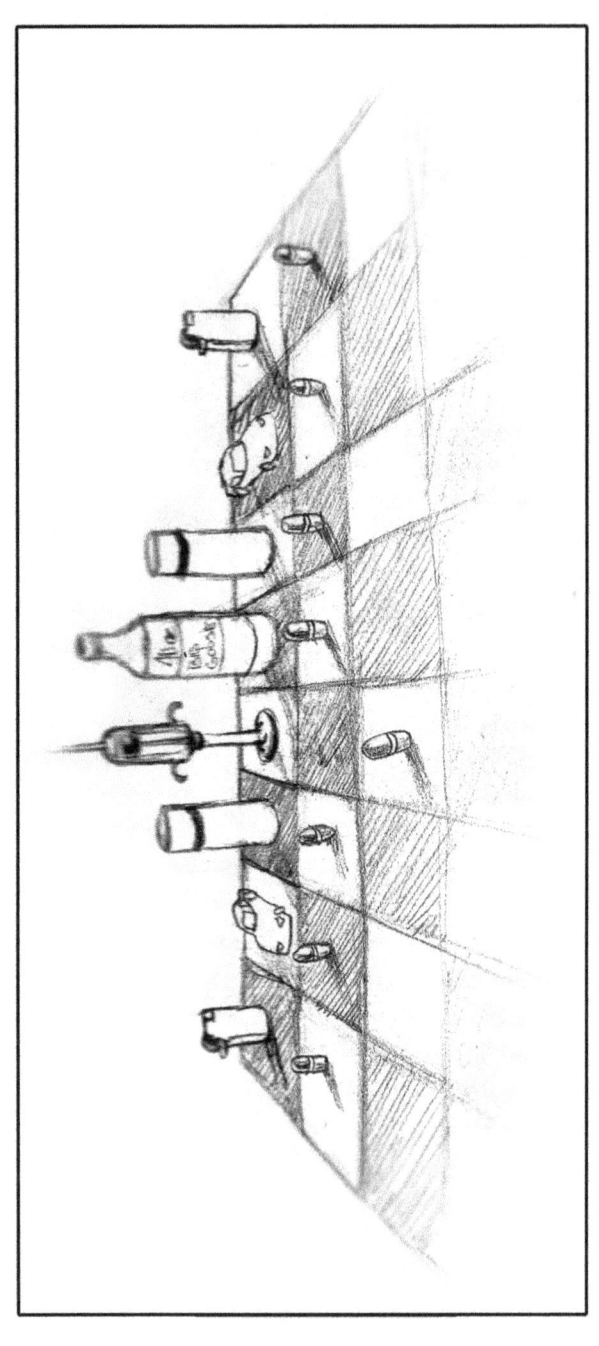

It was a Game

Written for eleventh grade students at
South Western High School
Inaugural Ceremony
November 2003

It was a deadly and more dangerous game
everyday
I didn't care about my reputation or what others had to say
Seduction is what I wanted
A game I wanted to play

Kissing, touching, and smooching with other
peoples physical entity
Logically, I didn't fear losing my virginity

A big price to pay
The game I wanted to play
Abortion had its way
I didn't want the game to end this way

That still wasn't enough to get my attention
I wanted a game extension
I acted as if I had no previous retention

Drugs and alcohol keep me in mental suspension
Male and female relationships keep me in tension

The game got hard
I began to feel the scars
My heart was left marred
I fought real hard

I wanted to die, I thought about suicide
After consideration, I didn't take the ride
I felt lonely inside
I no longer felt valued
So I wanted to hide

My friends didn't know that I getting deeper
Sorrow and pain was getting steeper
They thought I was okay because I was smoking the reefer
But I was screaming in a deep dark secret

No one knew that my game was over
I no longer wanted to play the female rover

I threw away the cigarettes and pour out the liquor
Stopped dating men that would pull the trigger

The DD's would no longer see me
Because I found the key to eternity
His name is Jesus you see

Hear the cry of the children

Watery eyes keep a rollin, as my hearts filled wit sorrow
All I wanna is for somebody to hear my cry
Don't understand whys I born, what the purpose of my life is
Lord, hear my cry

Been molested, feelin mighty alone,
Mamma gone, Daddy gone
I'm a just left
Place for dos orphans adopted me
Been molested and vowed I'd tell no body
Mines heart hurt'n, bleed'n in pain
Why's don't it ever change?
Lord, hear my cry

Why's it got to be dis way?
I wanna live in a world of play
Illusion and fantasy is my glory,
Cause no body understands my story

The voice I has when I's a child was killed
When I made a sound
Now I hope to close my lips in wishin I'd desist

Drugs and murder all's I know
How do I get out of dis hole?
Pits of hell round about fire, smoke, and death

Bars are strong to dat prison I hold can't open mine's heart,
I's feel so cold

Anybody out dare hear my cry?
The cry of death I feel I'd die
Anybody listen to da children's cry
A groan, a groan, deep wit in
A piercing cry of pain
Eyes filled wit tears and stain
Hearts feel'n weak and lame

Da children of tomorrow
Da children of the world
Whose once had a hope and dream
Now all's I hear is dat tormenting scream

Hear our cry oh Lord
The hurt goes deep wit in
Could it be our past generations?
Or could it be our sin?

A cry, a cry goes into your ears
A cry to be free
You oh Lord can help me, be me

Alcohol and dope is all around
A world of disillusionment that can only cause a frown
I's wrapped up and rolled up in dis world to try to be

I's reaching out wit only one breath saying
Lord, please help me

Babies cry, children's cry, we all cry alike
Do you hear the depth of our heart? Or is you sleep at night?
When's the time of our deliverance?
When's it gonna come?

Hear the cry of the children Lord,
Hear it when it comes

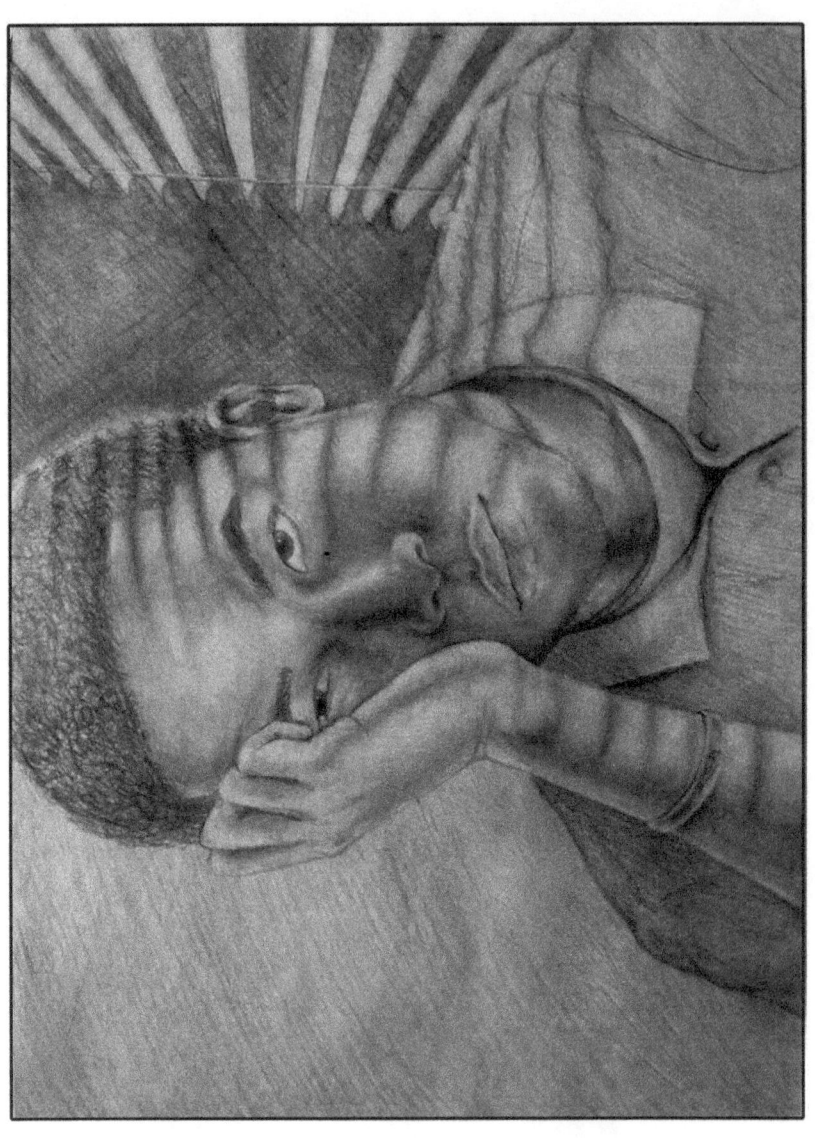

Is There Hope

Stretched out facing the opposition
Stunned by the blows of life
Dealt a hand that can't stand
Pierced inside, turned upside down
Looking everywhere, nothing nowhere

Sorrow, Sadness
Can't get out, can't go in
Lost expectation, no anticipation
Is there hope while I grope

Bars around
Steel encompassed about
No view, No way out
Need the keys
The hope of getting free
All I can see is what happened to me

Scrapping, Squealing
Fighting, Fussing
Feel like cussing

Not in a place where I want to be
Is there a place that I can see?
Is there hope?

Touching You

When I reached out to You
You were as liquid rain
You are the waters that flow over my head
Rivers that run through my soul
You touch but can't be physically touched
Your form is transparent
But I am rather touched by You
As I humble as a child, You cover me
In the shadows of Your wings I trust
It is You that made me, as this is true
You protect me
You shield me from the unseen world
I am in You
In the deep places of Your heart
In the expanse of Your glory
As the oceans cover the earth
I know in a moment in time
In time forever
That I am not alone

Always Faithful

In love and in truth
In sacrifice and in death
My soul I give
At the cross I rest
In my tears I travail
In my heart I prevail
Taking me to paths unseen
Giving me strengths unknown
In this I've grown
Courage to win
Boldness to obtain
Spirits undefeated
Lord, You reign!
In hell and in torment my soul prevails
You resurrect the righteous,
It's You we hail
In darkness and present death
We are not alone
In the days that lie ahead
We will always be faithful

Romance Me

Everyday I realize that I need you girl
To me a day without you is a day alone
When you call and when I see your face
Something in me lives
It's at that moment that I realize that I truly love you
I can't wait to hold you in my arms and kiss you
When I am with you nothing else matters
I feel an inward peace and an assurance that you are mine
Not just today, but forever and ever

Romance Me

When the cold of winter appears
I dream of logs on the fire
And you and me warming beside it
I think of big thick blankets
And you and I nestled together inside
Roasting marshmallows
Warming hot tea on the stove
As the crisp night air blows
I find myself looking for your touch
Looking for my man to embrace me tightly
I know that winter is only a season
And though the seasons change
The warmth of my love
Will always remain the same

Romance Me

There were many tough days,
Days, I thought we would not make it girl
But through it all you showed me
How strong our union really is

You are the most courageous woman I have ever met
It's your strength that carries me

Though there are millions of women in the world
Everything changes when I see you
Your beauty enraptures me year after year
And in time you just keep getting better and better

You are a dynamic wife, women, and mother
And if I had to marry you again, I would
Because there is no one else that makes me
Happier than you do
I love spending my life with you
Honey, I will always love you
You are the Romance of my life
And you always make me feel complete

Me too baby,
Romance Me

Other Books

Poiema, by Judith Peart: A collection of poetry written by Judith Peart; and illustrations by one of her sons Jeshua David Peart

Wisdom From Above, by Judith Peart: A biblically based booklet of quotes for practical living.

Sexual Healing, by Judith Peart, FOREWORD: "Your hearts will be touched, your feelings, and emotions challenged as you read this book ... Thank you Judith for your courage and transparency to help others as the Holy Spirit has helped you. Freely you have received. Freely you have given" (Dr. Sandra Phillips Hayden).

100 Never, by Judith Peart: Quotes to Help Women Improve Their Marriage Relationship

The Lamb, by Donald Peart: This book is a detailed look at the Lamb of God. He is King and Lord. We explore His wonderful character and work as it relates to our expected lifestyle, self-esteem and relational living. The book starts with His blood that "speaks better things."

Jesus' Resurrection, Our Inheritance, by Donald Peart: This book is a detailed look at the resurrection of Jesus Christ and the two phases associated with each of the four resurrections.

Sex Pleasures, By Donald Peart: This book is a detailed look at some of the vices of sexuality (apparent pleasures) that have damaged many, with the view to bring healing through the forgiveness of Jesus.

Forgiven 490, by Donald Peart w/Judith Peart: Jesus said "every sin and blasphemy shall be forgiven unto men," except for one particular blasphemy. Jesus wants to deliver all of mankind by forgiving us, and teaching us how to forgive others!

The Days of the Seventh Angel, By Donald Peart: A volume of the eschatology series that opens the mystery of God relative to the seventh angel who sounds the last trumpet.

The Torah (The Principle) of Giving, by Donald Peart: The text is a guide for those who desire to be a giver in the right way. It will release the bound from the curse of the law. Yet, the book will help the reader develop responsible giving.

The Time Came, by Donald Peart: The appearing of Jesus, in person, 2,000 years ago was the sign that that age was effectively over. The change of these ages *"into the age"* to come is also in a Person—*"the Lord's Christ,"* both head and body. Jesus **is** *"the beginning **and the end.**"*

The Last Hour, The First Hour, The Forty-Second Generation, by Donald Peart: This book explores the book of Revelations, the book of Daniel, the Gospels, and so on to unveil an understanding of times

Vision Real, by Donald Peart: What is real vision? Is vision animate or a real person?

The False Prophet, Alias, Another Beast V1, by Donald Peart is a comprehensive study manual that exposes "another beast," and his purpose.

"the beast" V2, by Donald Peart: "Then the angel said to me: " 'Why are you astonished? I will explain to you the mystery of …the beast….'"

Son of Man Prophesy Against the false prophet …," V2.1, by Donald Peart: This volume is a comprehensive instruction booklet that prophesies **against** "the false prophet," which is the spirit of Antichrist.

The Dragon's Tail (The Many False Prophets), V3, by Donald Peart: The seven headed dragon in the book of Revelation used his tail to fling. His seven heads are seven ruling angels—who dominate some so-called "elders…" His "tail" is a metaphor for the "many false prophets."

The Work of Lawlessness Revealed, by Donald Peart: a detailed look at the 2 Thessalonians 2, discussing topic like mystery of lawlessness, the man of sin who acts like God in the temple of God, etc.

When God Made Satan, by Donald Peart: a book that discusses the origin of Satan as opposed to Mr. and Mrs. Adam.

CROWN OF GLORY MINISTRIES
P.O. Box 1041 Randallstown, MD 21133
E-mail: secretary@crownofgloryministries.net
Secretary Phone: 410-905-0308